HOOKED HATS

HOOKED HATS
20 Easy Crochet Projects

MARGARET HUBERT

Creative Publishing
international

CHANHASSEN, MN

For my wonderful grandchildren, the sunshine of my life.

Acknowledgments

I wish to thank Alchemy Yarns of Transformation, Berroco, Inc., Lion Brand Yarn Company, Patons Yarns, Plymouth Yarn Company, and Tahki/Stacy Charles, Inc., who so graciously donated yarns for most of the projects in this book. I also wish to thank Jeannine Buehler for helping me crochet some of the hats.

Creative Publishing international

Copyright 2006
Creative Publishing international
18705 Lake Drive East
Chanhassen, Minnesota 55317
1-800-328-3895
www.creativepub.com
All rights reserved

President/CEO: Ken Fund

Vice President/Retail Sales: Kevin Haas

Executive Editor: Alison Brown Cerier

Senior Editor: Linda Neubauer

Photo Stylist: Joanne Wawra

Creative Director: Brad Springer

Photo Art Director: Tim Himsel

Photographers: Steve Galvin, Andrea Rugg, Jon Haglof

Production Manager: Laura Hokkanen

Cover Design: Dania Davey

Page Layout: Deborah Pierce

Printed in China
10 9 8 7 6 5 4 3 2 1

Library of Congress Cataloging-in-Publication Data
Hubert, Margaret.
   Hooked Hats : 20 easy crochet projects / Margaret Hubert.
      p. cm.
   ISBN 1-58923-256-9 (soft cover)
   1. Crocheting--Patterns.   I. Title.
TT825.H7985 2006
746.43'40432--dc22 2005035041

All the yarns used in this book can be found or ordered at your local yarn shop or craft store. Visit the following web sites for more information about the yarns shown:

Alchemy Yarns of Transformation
www.alchemyyarns.com

Berroco, Inc.
www.berrocco.com

Brown Sheep Company, Inc.
www.brownsheep.com

Caron International
www.caron.com

Katia Yarns/Knitting Fever
www.knittingfever.com

Lion Brand Yarn Company
www.lionbrand.com

On Line Yarns/Knitting Fever
www.knittingfever.com

Patons Yarns
www.patonsyarns.com

Plymouth Yarn Company
www.plymouthyarn.com

Sirdar Spinning Company
www.sirdar.co.uk

Tahki/Stacy Charles, Inc.
www.tahkistacycharles.com

Wool Pak Yarns NZ
www.baabajoeswool.com

Contents

About the Projects

A crocheted hat can be a hip beanie that a teen wears everywhere, or a pastel baby hat with a curlicue on top. It can be a big-brimmed hat for summer or a furry hood for the coldest day of winter. It can be super-bulky or lacey mesh, pretty or sophisticated. You will find all these kinds of hooked hats and many more in *Hooked Hats.*

I have designed twenty hats that are all fun, fast, and in fashion. All are easy, even if you are a beginner. Several hats are made using only single crochet. A multi-textured, multi-colored yarn can turn the most basic, single-crochet hat into a work of art! Other hats feature textural stitches that are easy to learn.

Some hats are worked in the round, beginning at the crown and working down to the brim. Other hats are cro-cheted in rows and sewn together in the back. If you need to learn or review a stitch, just go to the basics section at the back, which has detailed, photographed instructions.

For each hat, I chose a yarn to comple-ment the stitch and the style of the hat. Smooth cotton yarns are great for warm-weather hats and caps. They show off the texture of the crochet stitches and are good for decorative stitches like shells or popcorn, and they make even single crochet look fascinating. Hats made with cotton yarns also wear and wash well. For the Silky Cloche, I used a beautiful smooth silk yarn that shimmers in the light. Highly textured novelty yarns give a hat special character, but the stitches don't show, so I use simple stitches and let the yarn take center stage. For the Hot Textures Hat, a lovely ribbon yarn is com-bined with a highly textured acrylic yarn in a single crochet ribbing pattern to make it not only fun and interesting but also warm.

The wonderful new yarns offer many choices. You can make a hat lightweight and airy or warm and wooly, thick or thin, in natural colors or all the colors of the rainbow.

Give your hats personality by adding a flower or two or a special hatband. Tassels on earflaps, corkscrews on crowns, pom-poms on ties—mix and match elements.

The materials lists will tell you the weight and type of each yarn, as well as the brands and colors I used. You can substitute different yarns of the same weight and certainly choose your own colors.

While most crocheted hats have some "give" and will fit several sizes, it is still necessary to measure your head and check your gauge to ensure a good fit. For an accurate head measurement, place a tape measure across the forehead and, holding the tape snugly, measure around the full circumference of the head. Crochet a sample with your yarn and the hook size suggested to make sure your gauge matches the gauge listed. If you do not get the proper gauge, try a larger or smaller hook. You can also change the hook size to make a particular hat a little smaller or larger.

If you are new to crochet, I hope this book will help you learn the stitches and inspire you to hook one hat after another. If you are already hooked on crochet, I hope that you will enjoy my ideas and patterns. Enjoy watching each hat take shape and become a thing of beauty that you will be proud to wear or give.

Margaret Hubert is also the author of Hooked Bags, Hooked Throws, Hooked Scarves, How to Free-Form Crochet, *and six other books. She designs crochet projects for yarn companies and magazines and teaches at yarn shops, retreats, and national gatherings.*

Silky Cloche

This is a classic cloche to wear spring through fall.

You can wear the brim down or flipped up on the

front, side, or all around. Add flair with a bright

flower or a hatband if you like (see Hat

Embellishments on page 26).

YARN

Lightweight silk/wool blend yarn

Shown: Synchronicity by Alchemy, 50% silk 50% merino wool, 1.75 oz (50 g)/110 yd (101 m): Bronze #090M, 3 skeins

HOOKS

9/I (5.5 mm)

8/H (5 mm)

STITCH USED

Single crochet

GAUGE

$3\frac{1}{2}$ sc = 1" (2.5 cm) on 9/I hook

NOTIONS

Stitch marker

Tapestry needle

FINISHED SIZE

20" to 22" (51 to 56 cm) head circumference

Lightweight silk/wool blend yarn in single crochet.

HAT

Hat is worked with double strand throughout.

Foundation rnd: Using 9/I hook, ch 4, join with Sl st to form ring.

Rnd 1: Work 8 sc in ring, pm for beg of rnds, carry marker up at end of each rnd.

Rnd 2: Work 2 sc in each st around (16 sc).

Rnd 3: * Work 1 sc in next st, 2 sc in next st, rep from * around (24 sc).

Rnd 4: * Work 1 sc in each of next 2 sts, 2 sc in next st, rep from * around (32 sc).

Rnd 5: * Work 1 sc in each of next 3 sts, 2 sc in next st, rep from * around (40 sc).

Rnd 6: * Work 1 sc in each of next 4 sts, 2 sc in next st, rep from * around (48 sc).

Rnd 7: * Work 1 sc in each of next 5 sts, 2 sc in next st, rep from * around (56 sc).

Rnd 8: * Work 1 sc in each of next 6 sts, 2 sc in next st, rep from * around (64 sc).

Rnds 9–18: Work even.

Rnd 19 (first inc rnd): * Work 1 sc in each of next 3 sts, 2 sc in next st, rep from * around, end 2 sc in last st (80 sc).

Rnds 20–28: Work even.

Rnds 29–32: Change to 8/H hook. Work even.

Rnd 33 (second inc rnd): Change back to 9/I hook. * Work 1 sc in each of next 9 sts, 2 sc in next st, rep from * around (90 sc).

Rnds 34–41: Work even, end last rnd with Sl st, fasten off, weave in ends using tapestry needle.

Hot Textures Hat

Chunky, stylish hats are easy to make with today's textural yarns. This hat has twice the texture, since it's made with a smooth ribbon yarn and a nubby acrylic yarn hooked together. For even more surface interest, the pattern creates a ribbed effect by working single crochet stitches through the back loop on every row.

YARN

Bulky-weight ribbon yarn

Shown: Incredible by Lion Brand, 100% nylon, 1.75 oz (50 g)/110 yd (100 m): Purple Party #207, 2 balls

Bulky-weight acrylic yarn

Shown: Homespun by Lion Brand, 98% acrylic/2% polyester, 6 oz (170 g)/185 yd (170 m): Coral Gables #370, 1 skein

HOOK

10½/K (6.5 mm)

STITCHES USED

Single crochet

Single crochet through back loop

GAUGE

10 sc = 4" (10 cm)

NOTION

Tapestry needle

FINISHED SIZE

20" to 22" (51 to 56 cm) head circumference

Ribbed effect created by working single crochet through back loops.

HAT

Hat is worked with one strand of each yarn held together throughout.

Foundation row: Ch 45. Starting in second ch from hook, work 1 sc in each ch to end, ch 1, turn.

Row 1: Sk first st, * work 1 sc tbl in next st, rep from * across, work 1 sc in tch, ch 1, turn (44 sc). Rep row 1 for 9" (23 cm).

Begin crown shaping as follows:

Row 1: Sk first st, work 1 sc in next st * sc2tog, sc in next st, sc in next st, rep from * across (33 sc), ch 1, turn.

Row 2: Sk first st, * work 1 sc tbl in next st, rep from * across, work 1 sc in tch, ch 1, turn.

Row 3: Sk first st, sc2tog, * work 1 sc in next st, sc2tog, rep from * across, making last sc in tch (22 sc), ch 1, turn.

Rows 4 and 5: Rep row 2 of crown shaping.

Row 6: Sk first st, * sc2tog, rep from * across, end 1 sc (11 sc), fasten off, leaving long tail.

Ribbon yarn in reverse single crochet accents the brim edge.

FINISHING

1. With right side of brim facing, using ribbon yarn only, work one row of single crochet along edge, do not turn. Work one row of reverse single crochet across row, fasten off.

2. Thread the yarn tail onto a tapestry needle. Gather the remaining stitches at the top, but don't cut the yarn.

3. Sew the back seam and weave in ends.

Poodle Cap

This cuddly, head-hugging cap is made

with a novelty bouclé yarn. Hooked

entirely in single crochet, this is a

great project for beginners.

Super bulky bouclé yarn in single crochet.

YARN

Super bulky bouclé yarn

Shown: Pooch by Patons, 63% acrylic/27% wool/10% nylon, 2.4 oz (68 g)/36 yd (33 m): Indian Summer #65610, 1 ball

HOOK

10½/K (6.5 mm)

STITCH USED

Single crochet

GAUGE

6½ sc = 4" (10 cm)

NOTIONS

Stitch marker

Tapestry needle

FINISHED SIZE

20" to 21" (51 to 53.5 cm) head circumference

CAP

Foundation rnd: Ch 4, join with Sl st to form ring. Work 6 sc in center of ring, pm for beg of rnds, carry marker up at end of each rnd, do not join with Sl st after each rnd.

Rnd 1: Work 2 sc in each st (12 sc).

Rnd 2: * Work 1 sc in next st, 2 sc in next st, rep from * around (18 sc).

Rnd 3: * Work 1 sc in each of next 2 sts, 2 sc in next st, rep from * around (24 sc).

Rnd 4: * Work 1 sc in each of next 3 sts, 2 sc in next st, rep from * around (30 sc).

Rnd 5: * Work 1 sc in each of next 4 sts, 2 sc in next st, rep from * around (36 sc).

Rnds 6–11: Work 1 sc in each st around, fasten off, leaving a 4" (10 cm) length of yarn, weave in ends using tapestry needle.

Chenille Cloche

Chenille yarns are so soft and cozy. This cloche

has drama. You can add a crescent

embellishment (see page 26).

YARN
Super bulky weight
chenille yarn

Shown: Chenille Thick & Quick
by Lion Brand, 91% acrylic/9%
rayon, 100 yd (92 m): Grass
Green #130, 1 skein

HOOK
10½/K (6.5 mm)

STITCHES USED
Single crochet

Half double crochet

GAUGE
8 sc = 4" (10 cm)

NOTION
Tapestry needle

FINISHED SIZE
20" to 21" (51 to 53.5 cm)
head circumference

Chenille yarn in alternating rows of single crochet and half double crochet.

HAT

Foundation row: Ch 43. Starting in second ch from hook, work 1 sc in each ch to end, ch 2, turn.

Row 1: Sk first st (tch counts as first st now and throughout), * work 1 hdc in next st, rep from * across (42 hdc), ch 1, turn.

Row 2: Sk first st, * work 1 sc in next st, rep from * across (42 sc), ch 2, turn.

Rep rows 1 and 2 for 7" (18 cm) from beg, ending with sc row, ch 1, turn.

Crown of hat is worked entirely in sc.

First dec row: * Work 1 sc in each of next 12 sts, sc2tog, rep from * 2 times more (39 sc), ch 1, turn.

Second dec row: * Work 1 sc in each of next 7 sts, sc2tog, rep from * 3 times more, 1 sc, 1 sc in top of tch (35 sc), ch 1, turn.

Third dec row: Work 1 sc in each of next 2 sts, sc2tog, * sc in each of next 3 sts, sc2tog, rep from * 5 times (28 sc), ch 1, turn.

Work 1 row even, ch 1, turn.

Fourth dec row: * Work 1 sc in each of next 2 sts, sc2tog, rep from * (21 sc), ch 1, turn.

Work 1 row even, ch 1, turn.

Fifth dec row: * Work 1 sc in next st, sc2tog, rep from * (14 sc), ch 1, turn.

Work 1 row even, ch 1, turn.

Sixth dec row: Sc2tog across, fasten off, leaving long tail for sewing.

FINISHING

1. Thread the yarn tail onto a tapestry needle. Gather the remaining stitches at the top, but don't cut the yarn.

2. Sew the back seam and weave in ends.

3. Embellish with a spiral crescent (page 26), if desired.

Peach Cooler

This is a fresh style for spring and summer. The

brim can be folded up or rolled. It will hold its shape

because it is crocheted with two strands of cotton.

YARN

Lightweight cotton yarn in two colors

Shown: Cotton Classic by Tahki/Stacy Charles, 100% cotton, 1.75 oz (50 g)/108 yd (100 m): Dark Peach #3473, 2 skeins; Light Peach #3476, 2 skeins

HOOKS

9/I (5.5 mm)

6/G (4 mm)

STITCH USED

Single crochet

GAUGE

14 sc = 4" (10 cm) on 9/I hook

NOTIONS

Stitch marker

Tapestry needle

FINISHED SIZE

20" to 21" (51 to 53.5 cm) head circumference

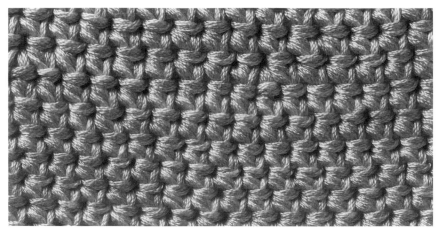

Two strands of lightweight cotton yarn in slightly different shades worked together in single crochet.

HAT

Hat is worked with one strand of each yarn held tog throughout. WS of sc is used as RS of hat.

Foundation rnd: Using 9/I hook, ch 4, join with Sl st to form ring. Work 8 sc in ring, pm after eighth st, do not join, do not ch, carry marker up at end of each rnd.

Rnd 1: * Work 2 sc in next st, rep from * around (16 sc).

Rnd 2: * Work 1 sc in next st, 2 sc in next st, rep from * around (24 sc).

Rnd 3: * Work 1 sc in each of next 2 sts, 2 sc in next st, rep from * around (32 sc).

Rnd 4: * Work 1 sc in each of next 3 sts, 2 sc in next st, rep from * around (40 sc).

Rnd 5: * Work 1 sc in each of next 4 sts, 2 sc in next st, rep from * around (48 sc).

Rnds 6 and 7: * Work 1 sc in next st, rep from * around (48 sc).

Rnd 8: * Work 1 sc in each of next 5 sts, 2 sc in next st, rep from * around (56 sc).

Rnds 9 and 10: Rep rnds 6 and 7.

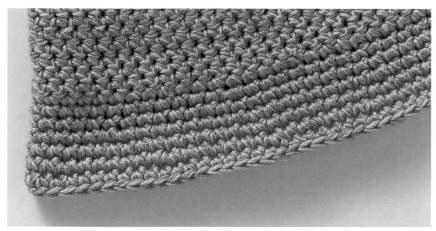

Rows of tight single crochet stitches cause the hat brim to roll.

Rnd 11: * Work 1 sc in each of next 6 sts, 2 sc in next st, rep from * around (64 sc).

Rnds 12 and 13: Rep rnds 6 and 7.

Rnd 14: * Work 1 sc in each of next 7 sts, 2 sc in next st, rep from * around (72 sc).

Rnds 15–28: Rep rnd 6, join with Sl st, and turn, reversing direction.

Start rolled brim as follows:

Rnd 29 (first inc row): * Work 1 sc in each of next 17 sts, 2 sc in next st, rep from * around (76 sc).

Rnd 30: Rep rnd 6.

Rnd 31 (second inc row): Work 1 sc in each of next 2 sts, * 1 sc in each of next 7 sts, 2 sc in next st, rep from * around, end sc in each of last 2 sts (85 sc).

Rnd 32: Rep rnd 6.

Rnd 33 (third inc row): Work 1 sc in next st, * 1 sc in each of next 6 sts, 2 sc in next st, rep from * around (99 sc).

Rnd 34: Change to 6/G hook. Rep rnd 6 (this tightens brim, causing it to roll up), fasten off, weave in ends using tapestry needle.

Hat Embellishments

You can dress up your hats with crocheted embellishments in contrasting colors and textures. Add a scalloped hatband to any of the cloches. Hook a flower or a wavy crescent to accent any of the close-fitting caps, cloches, or brimmed hats. Sew the flourishes in place or use safety pins for quick changes.

HATBAND

Hatband is worked with double strand throughout.

Foundation rnd: Using 9/I hook, ch 5, join with Sl st to form ring.

Work 6 hdc, ch 4, 1 hdc in ring. * Turn, ch 1, work 6 hdc, ch 4, 1 hdc in ch-4 sp. Rep from * until hatband is 22" (56 cm), fasten off, weave in ends using tapestry needle.

Using tapestry needle, sew ends tog. Attach hatband to hat.

CRESCENT

Foundation row: Using 10½/K hook, ch 14.

Row 1: Starting in 3rd ch from hook, work 1 hdc in each ch to end, turn.

Row 2: Ch 3, * work 3 dc in each st to end, fasten off, leaving a long tail for sewing.

Twist crescent into floral shape, sew together using tapestry needle, and weave in ends. Attach crescent to hat.

ROSE

Foundation rnd: Using 5/F hook, ch 4, join with Sl st to form ring.

Rnd 1: Work 12 sc in ring, join with Sl st to first sc, ch 1.

Rnd 2: Sc in same sc, * ch 3, sk 1, sc in next sc, rep from * around, end ch 3, sk 1 sc, and join in first st (7 lps).

Rnd 3: * In next ch lp, work [sc, hdc, 3 dc, hdc, sc], rep from * around, end Sl st in first sc, fasten off.

Rnd 4: Working in back of petals (in the skipped sc), join yarn in BL of sc on the second rnd below last and first petals, * ch 5, sc tbl of next sc on second rnd below next 2 petals, rep from * around, end ch 5, sc in joining st.

Rnd 5: In next ch lp, work [sc, hdc, 5 dc, hdc, sc], rep from * around, end Sl st in first sc, fasten off, weave in ends using tapestry needle. Attach rose to hat.

HAT EMBELLISHMENTS

YARN

Hatband: Lightweight silk/wool blend yarn

Shown: Synchronicity by Alchemy, 50% silk/50% merino wool, 1.75 oz (50 g)/110 yd (101 m): Bronze #090M, 3 skeins

Crescent: Super bulky weight chenille yarn

Shown: Chenille Thick & Quick by Lion Brand, 91% acrylic/9% rayon, 100 yd (92 m): Grass Green #130, 1 skein

Rose: Medium weight ribbon yarn

Shown: Berroco Glacé, 100% rayon, 1.75 oz (50 g)/75 yd (69 m): Shock #2518

HOOKS

Hatband: 9/I (5.5 mm)
Crescent: 10½/K (6.5 mm)
Rose: 5/F (3.75 mm)

STITCHES USED

Single crochet
Single crochet through back loop
Double crochet
Half double crochet

GAUGE

Varies with yarn and hook

NOTION

Tapestry needle

FINISHED SIZES

Hatband: 22" (56 cm)
Crescent: 3" (7.5 cm)
Rose: 3" (7.5 cm)

Mesh Cap

An open-work mesh cap has lots of attitude. If you love this downtown look, hook it in lots of colors including natural cotton.

YARN

Medium-weight cotton/rayon blend yarn

Shown: Cotton Twist by Berroco, 70% cotton/30% rayon, 1.75 oz (50 g)/85 yd (78 m): Crème Fraiche #8374, 1 skein

HOOK

6/G (4 mm)

STITCHES USED

Single crochet

Double crochet

Reverse single crochet

GAUGE

7 dc, 6 ch-2 sp = 4" (10 cm)

NOTION

Tapestry needle

FINISHED SIZE

20" to 21" (51 to 53.5 cm) head circumference

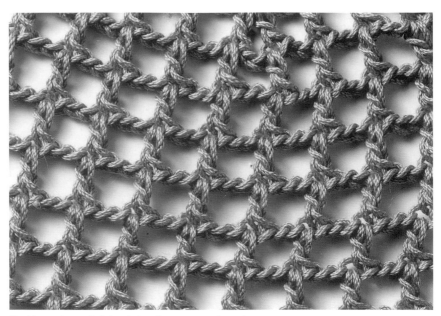

Double crochet and chain stitches form open-work mesh.

Foundation rnd: Ch 4, join with Sl st to form ring. Ch 4, (counts as dc, ch 1), work [dc, ch 1] in ring 7 times (8 dc), join with Sl st to third ch of beg ch 4.

Rnd 1: Ch 5 (counts as 1 dc, ch 2, now and throughout), work 1 dc in same st, ch 2, * [1 dc, ch 2, 1 dc] in next st (inc made), ch 2, rep from * around, join with Sl st to third ch of beg ch 5 (16 dc).

Rnd 2: Ch 5, work 1 dc in same st, ch 2, 1 dc in next st, ch 2, * [1 dc, ch 2, 1 dc] in next st (inc made), ch 2, 1 dc next st, ch 2, rep from * around, join with Sl st to third ch of beg ch 5 (24 dc).

Rnd 3: Ch 5, work 1 dc in same st, ch 2, 1 dc in next st, ch 2, 1 dc in next st, ch 2, * [1 dc, ch 2, 1 dc] in next st (inc made), ch 2, 1 dc in next st, ch 2, 1 dc in next st, ch 2, rep from * around, join with Sl st to third ch of beg ch 5 (32 dc).

Rnd 4: Ch 5, * work 1 dc in next st, ch 2, rep from * around, join with Sl st to third ch of beg ch 5.

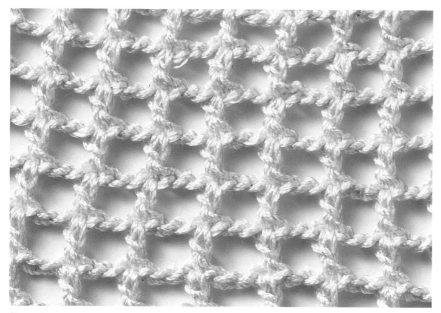

Shown in a natural color. The rayon fibers in the blended yarn have a soft luster.

Rnds 5–15: Rep rnd 4.

Rnd 16: Ch 1, * work 2 sc in next ch-2 sp, rep from * around, join with Sl st to beg ch 1.

Rnd 17: Work rev sc back over all sts of rnd 16, fasten off, weave in ends using tapestry needle.

Summer Breeze Brimmed Hat

Sometimes it's all about the stitch. This hat is all about the shell stitch. Hooked with two strands of yarn throughout to give it body, this hat has a slight brim to keep the sun off your face.

YARN

Medium-weight cotton/rayon blend yarn

Shown: Cotton Twist by Berroco, 70% cotton/30% rayon, 1.75 oz (50 g)/85 yd (78 m): Corot #8339, 4 skeins

HOOKS

6/G (4 mm)

8/H (5 mm)

STITCHES USED

Single crochet

Single crochet through back loop

Double crochet

Shell stitch

GAUGE

3 shell clusters = 4" (10 cm) on 6/G hook

2 shell clusters = 4" (10 cm) on 8/H hook

NOTIONS

Stitch marker

Tapestry needle

FINISHED SIZE

20" to 21" (51 to 53.5 cm) head circumference

33

Clusters of double crochet stitches form asymetrical shells.

HAT

Yarn is used double strand throughout.

Foundation rnd: Using 6/G hook, ch 4, join with Sl st to form ring. Work 8 sc in ring, pm for beg of rnds, carry marker up at end of each rnd.

Rnd 1: * Work 2 sc in next st, rep from * around (16 sc).

Rnd 2: * Work 1 sc in next st, 2 sc in next st, rep from * around (24 sc).

Rnd 3: * Work 1 sc in each of next 2 sts, 2 sc in next st, rep from * around (32 sc).

Rnd 4: * Work 1 sc in each of next 3 sts, 2 sc in next st, rep from * around (40 sc).

Rnd 5: * Work 1 sc in each of next 4 sts, 2 sc in next st, rep from * around (48 sc).

Rnd 6: * Work 1 sc in each of next 5 sts, 2 sc in next st, rep from * around (56 sc).

Rnd 7: * Work 1 sc in each of next 6 sts, 2 sc in next st, rep from * around (64 sc).

Rnd 8: * Work 1 sc in each of next 7 sts, 2 sc in next st, rep from * around (72 sc), join with Sl st, cont carry marker up after each rnd. Begin asymmetrical shell pattern as follows:

Rnd 9: Ch 3, sk 3 sts, * work [4 dc, ch 2, 1 dc] in next st, sk 4 sts, rep from * 13 times, join with Sl st to top of beg ch 3 (14 shell sts), ch 3, turn.

Rnd 10: * Work [4 dc, ch 2, 1 dc] in next ch-2 sp, rep from * 13 times, join with Sl st to top of of beg ch 3 (14 shell sts), ch 3, turn.

Rnds 11 and 12: Rep rnd 10, at end on rnd 12, ch 1 instead of 3, turn.

Rnd 13: Work 2 sc in first ch-2 sp, * 1 sc in each of next 4 sts, 1 sc in next ch-2 sp, rep from * around (72 sc), do not join, do not turn, cont carry marker.

Rnds 14 and 15: Sc tbl in each st around. At end of rnd 15, join with Sl st to first st of rnd, do not turn.

Rnd 16: Rep rnd 9.

Rnd 17: Rep rnd 10.

Rnd 18: Change to 8/H hook. Rep rnd 10, do not turn.

Rnd 19: * Work 1 sc in each of next 4 sts, 2 sc in ch-2 sp, rep from * around (84 sc).

Rnds 20 and 21: Sc tbl in each st around.

Rnd 22: Rep rnd 9 (16 shells).

Rnd 23: Rep rnd 10, end ch 1 instead of 3, turn.

Rnd 24: * Work 1 sc in each of next 4 sts, 2 sc in ch-2 sp, rep from * around, join with Sl st to beg ch 1, fasten off, weave in ends using tapestry needle.

Weaving Ribbon Cloche

Bright contrasting colors really pop. This is a low-fitting cloche with a row of eyelets that holds a crocheted ribbon. Change the ribbon to change the look. You can even make a ribbon out of a fun fur yarn.

YARN

Medium-weight cotton yarn for hat

Shown: Cotton Classic II by Tahki/Stacy Charles, 100% cotton, 1.75 oz (50 g)/ 74 yd (68 m): #2924, 2 skeins

Lightweight cotton yarn for ribbon

Shown: Cotton Classic by Tahki/Stacy Charles, 100% cotton, 1.75 oz (50 g)/108 yd (100 m): #3760, 1 skein

HOOKS

$10^{1}/_{2}$/K (6.5 mm) for hat

9/I (5.5 mm) for ribbon

STITCHES USED

Single crochet

Double crochet

GAUGE

8 dc = 4" (10 cm) on $10^{1}/_{2}$/K hook

NOTION

Tapestry needle

FINISHED SIZE

20" to 21" (51 to 53.5 cm) head circumference

37

Two strands of medium-weight cotton yarn in double crochet.

HAT
Yarn is used double strand throughout.

Foundation rnd: Using 10¹/₂/K hook, ch 4, join with Sl st to form ring. Work 9 sc in ring, join with Sl st.

Rnd 1: Ch 3 (counts as dc now and throughout), work 1 dc in same st as ch 3, 2 dc in each sc around (18 dc), join with Sl st to top of beg ch 3.

Rnd 2: Ch 3, sk first st, * work 2 dc in next st, 1 dc in next st, rep from * around, 2 dc in same st as beg ch 3 (27 dc), join with Sl st to top of beg ch 3.

Rnd 3: Ch 3, sk first st, work 1 dc in next st, * 2 dc in next st, 1 dc in each of next 2 sts, rep from * 7 times, 2 dc in same st as beg ch 3 (36 dc), join with Sl st to top of beg ch 3.

Rnd 4: Ch 3, sk first st, work 1 dc in next 2 sts, * 2 dc in next st, 1 dc in each of next 3 sts, rep from * 7 times, 2 dc in same st as beg ch 3 (45 dc), join with Sl st to top of beg ch 3.

Rnd 5: Ch 3, sk first st, work 1 dc in each st around, 1 dc in same st as beg ch 3 (45 dc), join with Sl st to top of beg ch 3.

Rep rnd 5 for 6¹/₂" (16.3 cm) from beg.

Open-work rnd: Ch 4 (counts as 1 dc, ch 1), sk st that ch 3 is coming from, sk next st, work 1 dc in next st, * ch 1, sk 1, 1 dc in next st, rep from * around, join with Sl st to third ch of beg ch 4, ch 1.

Open-work round creates holes for weaving ribbon.

Begin brim as follows:

Rnd 1: * Work 1 sc in ch-1 sp, 1 sc in next st, rep from * around (45 sc), join with Sl st to beg ch 1, ch 1.

Rnd 2: Sk first st, work 1 sc in each st around, join with Sl st to beg ch 1, ch 1.

Rnd 3: Sk first st, work 1 sc in each of next 7 sts, 2 sc in next st (inc made), * sc in each of next 8 sts, inc in next st, rep from * around (50 sc), join with Sl st to beg ch 1, ch 1.

Rnd 4: Sk first st, work 1 sc in each of next 8 sts, inc in next st, * sc in each of next 9 sts, inc in next st, rep from * around (55 sc), join with Sl st to beg ch 1, ch 1.

Rnd 5: Sk first st, work 1 sc in each of next 9 sts, inc in next st, * sc in each of next 10 sts, inc in next st, rep from * around (60 sc), fasten off, weave in ends using tapestry needle.

RIBBON
Foundation row: Using 9/I hook and 1 strand of lightweight yarn, ch 5. Starting in second ch from hook, work 1 sc in each ch, ch 1, turn.

Row 1: Sk first st, 1 sc in each st to end, ch 1, turn.

Rep row 1 for 36" (91.5 cm), fasten off, weave in ends using tapestry needle.

FINISHING
Weave ribbon in and out of open-work row, overlap and tie ends.

New Plaid Tam

Everyone is mad about plaid, and a jaunty tam is

the ultimate plaid accessory. Did you know you

could make plaid with crochet? The raised bars on

this hat are made with front post double crochet.

Don't be intimidated; you'll pick up the pattern

quickly once you start.

YARN

Medium-weight acrylic yarn

Shown: Simply Soft Brites by Caron, 100% acrylic, 6 oz (170 g)/315 yd (290 m): Blue Mint #9608, 1 skein (MC)

Bulky-weight ribbon yarn

Shown: On Line Linie, 100% polyacrylic, 1.75 oz (50 g)/100 yd (92 m): Space #114, 1 skein (CC)

HOOKS

6/G (4 mm)

9/I (5.5 mm)

10/J (6 mm)

STITCHES USED

Single crochet

Half double crochet

Front post double crochet

Reverse single crochet

GAUGE

16 sc = 4" (10 cm) on 6/G hook

14 hdc = 4" (10 cm) on 9/I hook

11 hdc = 4" (10 cm) on 10/J hook

NOTIONS

Stitch marker

Tapestry needle

8" (20.5 cm) piece of cardboard

FINISHED SIZE

20" (51 cm) head circumference

41

Ribbon yarn in single crochet forms raised bars in the plaid design.

HAT

Foundation rnd: Using 6/G hook and MC, starting with band, ch 76. Being careful not to twist, join with Sl st to form ring. Using a CC yarn, pm.

Rnd 1: Sc in each ch around, carry up marker now and at end of every rnd of band.

Rnd 2: Sc in each st around.

Rnds 3, 4, and 5: Rep rnd 2.

Rnd 6: Work 1 sc in first st, 2 sc in next st (inc made), * sc in each of next 8 sts, inc in next st, rep from * 7 times more, sc in each of last 2 sts (85 sc). End of band.

Change to 9/I hook and begin crown as follows:

Rnd 1: Ch 2 (counts as first hdc now and throughout), work 1 hdc in each st around (85 hdc), join with Sl st to top of beg ch 2.

Rnd 2: Ch 2, work 1 hdc in each of next 5 sts, * 1 FPdc over next hdc, 1 hdc in next st, 1 FPdc over next hdc, 1 hdc in each of next 11 sts, rep from * 4 times more, 1 FPdc over next hdc, 1 hdc in next st, 1 FPdc over next hdc, 1 hdc in each of next 6 sts, join with Sl st to top of beg ch 2, join CC, ch 2 (at end of this rnd, there will be 6 hdc at beg, 6 raised ribs with 11 hdc bet, 6 hdc at end).

Rnd 3: With CC, rep rnd 2, ch 2 with MC.

Rnds 4–7: Change to 10/J hook. With MC, rep rnd 2. At end of rnd 7, ch 2 with CC.

Rnd 8: With CC, rep rnd 2, ch 2 with MC.

Rnd 9 (first dec row): With MC, ch 2, work 1 hdc in each of next 3 sts, dec over next 2 sts (to dec, hdc, yo pick up lp in next st, yo pick up lp in next st, yo through all 5 lps on hook), * 1 FPdc over next FPdc, 1 hdc next st, 1 FPdc over next FPdc, dec over next 2 sts, 1 hdc in each of next 7 sts, dec over next 2 sts, rep from * 4 times, 1 FPdc, 1 hdc, 1 FPdc, dec over next 2 sts, 1 hdc in each of rem 4 sts, join with Sl st to top of beg ch 2 (73 sts).

Rnd 10: With MC, foll patt as established.

Rnd 11 (second dec row): With MC, dec 1 st before and after each raised rib (61 sts).

Rnd 12: With MC, foll patt as established.

Rnd 13 (3rd dec row): With CC, dec 1 st before and after each raised rib (49 sts).

Rnd 14: With MC, foll patt as established.

Rnd 15 (4th dec row): With MC, dec 1 st before and after each raised rib (37 sts).

Rnd 16: With MC, foll patt as established.

Rnd 17 (5th dec row): With MC, ch 2, work 1 FPdc, 1 hdc, 1 FPdc, * dec over next 2 sts , 1 hdc, 1 FPdc, 1 hdc, 1 FPdc, rep from * ending with Sl st to top of beg ch 2.

Rnd 18: With CC, ch 2, foll patt as established.

Rnd 19: With MC, ch 2, * work 1 FPdc, 1 hdc, 1 FPdc, 1 hdc, rep from * ending with Sl st in top of beg ch 2.

Rnd 20: With MC, ch 2, * work 1 FPdc, sk hdc, rep from * ending with Sl st in top of beg ch 2, fasten off, leaving an 18" (46 cm) end.

FINISHING

1. Using tapestry needle, draw long end through top of last row and pull up tight, knot, fasten off, weave in ends.
2. With CC and 9/I hook, work sc from top to bottom over each row of FPdc, forming vertical rows of plaid, weave in ends.
3. With MC and 6/G hook, work 1 row of sc and 1 row of rev sc around bottom of band, weave in ends.
4. To create tassel, wrap ribbon around an 8" (20.5 cm) piece of cardboard about 15 times. Thread a piece of ribbon under the loops at the top and tie tightly. Slip the loops off the cardboard. Tie another piece of ribbon around the loops 1" (2.5 cm) down from the top. Cut the loops at the other end. Tie the tassel to the cap point.

Simple Stuff Beanie

Beanies are on snowboarders, skateboarders, and lots of other teens and twenties who just like the look. Here is the first of three styles of this simple, close-fitting cap, which is sometimes called a skullcap or a bicycle hat. This first style has narrow stripes.

YARN

Medium-weight acrylic yarn

Shown: Canadiana by Patons, 100% acrylic, 3.5 oz (100g)/201 yd (185 m): Denim #00303, 1 skein (MC); Stonewash #00305, 1 skein (CC)

HOOK

9/I (5.5 mm)

STITCHES USED

Single crochet
Double crochet

GAUGE

12 dc = 4" (10 cm)

NOTION

Tapestry needle

FINISHED SIZE

20" to 22" (51 to 56 cm) head circumference

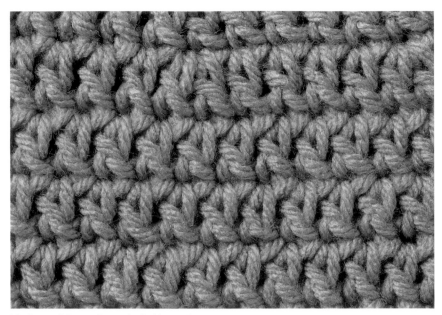

Medium-weight acrylic yarn in double crochet.

CAP

Foundation rnd: With MC, ch 4, join with Sl st to form ring.

Rnd 1: Ch 3 (counts as dc now and throughout), work 9 dc in ring, join with Sl st to top of beg ch 3.

Rnd 2: Ch 3, work 1 dc in same st as ch 3, 2 dc in each rem st around, join with Sl st to top of beg ch 3 (20 dc).

Rnd 3: Ch 3, work 2 dc in next st, * 1 dc in next st, 2 dc in next st, rep from * around, join with Sl st to top of beg ch 3 (30 dc).

Rnd 4: Ch 3, work 1 dc in next st, 2 dc in next st, * 1 dc in each of next 2 sts, 2 dc in next st, rep from * around, join with Sl st to top of beg ch 3 (40 dc).

Rnd 5: Ch 3, work 1 dc in each of next 2 sts, 2 dc in next st, * 1 dc in each of next 3 sts, 2 dc in next st, rep from * around, join with Sl st to top of beg ch 3 (50 dc).

Rnd 6: Ch 3, work 1 dc in each of next 3 sts, 2 dc in next st, * 1 dc in each of next 4 sts, 2 dc in next st, rep from * around, join with Sl st to top of beg ch 3 (60 dc).

Rnds 7–11: Ch 3, work 1 dc in each st around, join with Sl st to top of beg ch 3, do not fasten off MC.

Rnds 12 and 13: With CC, ch 1 (counts as sc now and throughout), sk first st, work 1 sc in each st around, join with Sl st to beg ch 1.

Rnds 14 and 15: With MC, rep rnds 12 and 13.

Rnds 16 and 17: With CC, rep rnds 12 and 13, fasten off.

FINISHING
Weave in ends using tapestry needle.

Girl Beanie

The girls like beanies, too, so this one is

styled for them.

YARN

Lightweight wool/acrylic blend yarn in two colors

Shown: Salsa DK by Sirdar, 50% merino wool/50% acrylic, 1.75 oz (50 g)/162 yd (149 m): Bright Orange #729, 1 ball (MC); Bright Blue #727, 1 ball (CC)

HOOK

9/I (5.5 mm)

STITCHES USED

Single crochet
Double crochet

GAUGE

12 dc = 4" (10 cm)

NOTION

Tapestry needle

FINISHED SIZE

20" to 22" (51 to 56 cm) head circumference

Lightweight wool/acrylic blend yarn in double crochet.

CAP

Foundation rnd: Using MC, ch 4, join with Sl st to form ring.

Rnd 1: Ch 3 (counts as dc now and throughout), work 9 dc in ring, join with Sl st to top of beg ch 3.

Rnd 2: Ch 3, work 1 dc in same st as ch 3, 2 dc in each rem st around, join with Sl st to top of beg ch 3 (20 dc).

Rnd 3: Ch 3, work 2 dc in next st, * 1 dc in next st, 2 dc in next st, rep from * around, join with Sl st to top of beg ch 3 (30 dc).

Rnd 4: Ch 3, work 1 dc in next st, 2 dc in next st, * 1 dc in each of next 2 sts, 2 dc in next st, rep from * around, join with Sl st to top of beg ch 3 (40 dc).

Rnd 5: Ch 3, work 1 dc in each of next 2 sts, 2 dc in next st, * 1 dc in each of next 3 sts, 2 dc in next st, rep from * around, join with Sl st to top of beg ch 3 (50 dc).

Rnd 6: Ch 3, work 1 dc in each of next 3 sts, 2 dc in next st, * 1 dc in each of next 4 sts, 2 dc in next st, rep from * around, join with Sl st to top of beg ch 3 (60 dc).

Rnds 7–11: Ch 3, work 1 dc in each st around, join with Sl st to top of beg ch 3, do not fasten off MC.

Rnd 12: With CC, ch 1 (counts as sc now and throughout), sk first st, work 1 sc in each st around, join with Sl st to beg ch 1.

Rnd 13: With MC, rep rnd 12.

Rnds 14–18: Rep rnds 12 and 13, fasten off.

FINISHING
Weave in ends using tapestry needle.

Big Stripes Beanie

This cap has wide stripes and an interesting texture created by crocheting through the back loop of the stitches. You can never have enough caps!

YARN

Medium-weight acrylic yarn in three colors

Shown: Canadiana by Patons, 100% acrylic, 3.5 oz (100g)/201 yd (185 m): Light Blue #00029, 1 skein (A); Denim #00303, 1 skein (B); Stonewash #00305, 1 skein (C)

HOOK

9/I (5.5 mm)

STITCHES USED

Single crochet

Double crochet

Double crochet through back loop

GAUGE

12 dc = 4" (10 cm)

NOTION

Tapestry needle

FINISHED SIZE

20" to 22" (51 to 56 cm) head circumference

Medium-weight acrylic yarn in double crochet worked through back loop.

CAP

Foundation rnd: Using A, ch 4, join with Sl st to form ring.

Rnd 1: Ch 3 (counts as dc now and throughout), work 9 dc in ring, join with Sl st to top of beg ch 3.

Rnd 2: Ch 3, working tbl of each st now and throughout, 1 dc in same st as ch 3, 2 dc in each rem st around, join with Sl st to top of beg ch 3 (20 dc).

Rnd 3: Ch 3, work 2 dc in next st, * 1 dc in next st, 2 dc in next st, rep from * around, join with Sl st to top of beg ch 3 (30 dc).

Rnd 4: Ch 3, work 1 dc in next st, 2 dc in next st, * 1 dc in each of next 2 sts, 2 dc in next st, rep from * around, join with Sl st to top of beg ch 3 (40 dc), fasten off A.

Rnd 5: Join B, ch 3, work 1 dc in each of next 2 sts, 2 dc in next st, * 1 dc in each of next 3 sts, 2 dc in next st, rep from * around, join with Sl st to top of beg ch 3 (50 dc).

Rnd 6: Ch 3, work 1 dc in each of next 3 sts, 2 dc in next st, * 1 dc in each of next 4 sts, 2 dc in next st, rep from * around, join with Sl st to top of beg ch 3 (60 dc).

Rnds 7 and 8: Ch 3, work 1 dc in each st around, join with Sl st to top of beg ch 3, fasten off B.

Rnds 9–11: Join C at beg of rnd 9, rep rnd 7, but do not fasten off C.

Rnds 12–18: Ch 1 (counts as sc now and throughout), sk first st, work 1 sc in each st around, join with Sl st to beg ch 1, fasten off C.

FINISHING
Weave in ends using tapestry needle.

Retro Stocking Cap

Stocking caps are back. They're just as much fun now as they were when kids spent their winter afternoons building snowmen and flying down hills on their wooden sleds. Here is a classic striped stocking cap, tassel and all.

YARN

Lightweight wool/acrylic blend yarn in two colors

Shown: Salsa DK by Sirdar, 50% merino wool/50% acrylic, 1.75 oz (50 g)/162 yd (149 m): Bright Blue #727, 1 ball (A); Bright Orange #729, 1 ball (B)

HOOK

6/G (4 mm)

STITCHES USED

Single crochet

Reverse single crochet

GAUGE

16 sc = 4" (10 cm)

NOTIONS

Stitch marker

Tapestry needle

8" (20.5 cm) piece of cardboard

FINISHED SIZE

18" to 20" (46 to 51 cm) head circumference

Rows of single crochet in alternating colors form stripes.

CAP

Foundation rnd: Using A, ch 3, join with Sl st to form ring.

Rnd 1: Work 4 sc in ring, pm for beg of rnds, carry marker up at end of each rnd.

Rnd 2: Work 1 sc in each st around.

Rnd 3: Work 2 sc in each st around (8 sc).

Rnds 4–7: Rep rnd 2.

Rnd 8: Work 2 sc in each st around (16 sc), do not fasten off A.

Rnd 9: Join B, work 1 sc in each st around, do not fasten off B.

Rnd 10: With A, work 1 sc in each st around, do not fasten off A.

Rnd 11: With B, work 1 sc in each st around, fasten off B.

Rnds 12–18: With A, work 1 sc in each st around.

Rnds 19–21: Rep rnds 9–11.

Rnd 22: With A, * work 1 sc in next st, 2 sc in next st, rep from * around (24 sc).

Rnds 23–28: Work 1 sc in each st around.

Rnds 29–31: Rep rnds 9–11.

Rnd 32: With A, * work 1 sc in each of next 2 sts, 2 sc in next st, rep from * around (32 sc).

Rnds 33–38: Work 1 sc in each st around.

Rnds 39–41: Rep rnds 9–11.

Rnd 42: With A, * work 1 sc in each of next 3 sts, 2 sc in next st, rep from * around (40 sc).

Rnds 43–48: Work 1 sc in each st around.

Rnds 49–51: Rep rnds 9–11.

Rnds 52–58: With A, work 1 sc in each st around.

Rnds 59–68: Rep rnds 49–58 once.

Rnds 69–77: Rep rnds 49–57.

Rnd 78: With A, * work 1 sc in each of next 4 sts, 2 sc in next st, rep from * around (48 sc).

Rnds 79–81: Rep rnds 9–11.

Rnd 82: With A, * work 1 sc in each of next 5 sts, 2 sc in next st, rep from * around (56 sc).

Rnds 83–87: Work 1 sc in each st around.

Rnd 88: * Work 1 sc in each of next 6 sts, 2 sc in next st, rep from * around (64 sc).

Rnds 89–91: Rep rnds 9–11.

Rnds 92–98: With A, work 1 sc in each st around.

Rnds 99–101: Rep rnds 9–11.

FINISHING

1. After last round, join a strand of A with B and, using both colors, work 1 round reverse single crochet, fasten off, and weave in ends using tapestry needle.

2. To create tassel, hold both colors together, and wrap yarn around an 8" (20.5 cm) piece of cardboard about 30 times. Thread a piece of yarn under the loops at the top and tie tightly. Slip the loops off the cardboard. Tie another piece of yarn around the loops 1" (2.5 cm) down from the top. Cut the loops at the other end. Tie the tassel to the cap point.

Tassel adds the finishing touch.

The Newsboy

Extra, extra, read all about it! This is an urban look with lots of attitude. The Newsboy has a great ribbed texture. The reverse side of the stitches is actually on the outside (thanks to Johnny, who told me it looked cooler that way). The ribs are formed by front post double crochet stitches, and the double crochet stitches between the ribs are worked in the spaces rather than the stitches. The bill is worked with two strands of yarn for extra stiffness.

YARN

Bulky-weight wool yarn

Shown: 14 Ply by Wool Pak Yarns NZ, 100% wool, 8 oz (250 g)/310 yd (285 m): Goldstone #27, 1 skein

HOOK

9/I (5.5 mm)

STITCHES USED

Single crochet

Double crochet

Front post double crochet

GAUGE

10 dc = 4" (10 cm)

NOTION

Tapestry needle

FINISHED SIZE

20" to 21" (51 to 53.5 cm) head circumference

Ribs formed by front post double crochet stitches; wrong side out.

BILL

Wind off about 12 yd (11 m) of yarn. Hold this yarn together with main skein to crochet bill with a double strand as follows:

Foundation row: Ch 27. Beg in second ch from hook, work 1 sc in each ch to end (26 sc), ch 1, turn.

Rows 1 and 2: Sk first st, * work 1 sc in next st, rep from * across, end 1 sc in tch, ch 1, turn.

Row 3: Sk first st, sc2tog, sc to last 3 sts, sc2tog, sc in last st (24 sc), ch 1, turn.

Row 4: Rep row 3 (22 sc).

Row 5: Rep row 3 (20 sc), fasten off, leaving a long end for sewing. Set cap bill aside.

CAP

Foundation rnd: Ch 4, join with Sl st to form ring, ch 3 (counts as dc now and throughout), work 15 dc in ring (16 dc), join with Sl st to top of ch 3.

Rnd 1: Ch 3, * work 1 FPdc in each of next 2 sts, 1 dc in sp bet last dc worked and next dc (inc made), rep from * 6 times more, 1 FPdc in each of next 2 sts, join with Sl st to top of beg ch 3 (24 dc).

Rnd 2: Ch 3, work 1 dc in next sp, 1 FPdc in each of next 2 FPdc, * 1 dc in next sp, sk dc, 1 dc in next sp, 1 FPdc in each of next 2 FPdc, rep from * 6 times more, join with Sl st to top of beg ch 3 (32 dc).

Rnd 3: Ch 3, work 1 dc in each of next 2 sps, 1 FPdc in each of next 2 FPdc, * 1 dc in each of next 3 sps, 1 FPdc in each of next 2 FPdc, rep from * 6 times more, join with Sl st to top of beg ch 3 (40 dc).

Rnd 4: Ch 3, work 1 dc in each of next 3 sps, 1 FPdc in each of next 2 FPdc, * 1 dc in each of next 4 sps, 1 FPdc in each of next 2 FPdc, rep from * 6 times more, join with Sl st to top of beg ch 3 (48 dc).

Cont to work patt as established, always having 1 more dc bet FPdc ribs, until you have 96 sts.

First dec row: Ch 3, sk 1 sp, dc dec in next 2 sps, 1 dc in each of next 4 sps, 1 dc dec in next 2 sps, 1 dc in next space, 1 FPdc in each of next 2 FPdc, * sk 1 sp, 1 dc next sp, dc dec in next 2 sps, 1 dc in each of next 4 sps, dc dec in next 2 sps, 1 dc in next sp, 1 FPdc in each of next 2 FPdc, rep from * around, join with Sl st to top of beg ch 3 (80 dc).

Second dec row: Ch 3, dc dec in next 2sps, 1 dc in each of next 3 sps, 1 dc dec in next 2 sps, sk 1 sp, 1 FPdc in each of next 2 FPdc, * 1 dc dec in next sp, 1 dc in each of next 3 sps, 1 dc dec in next 2sps, sk 1 sp dec, 2 FPdc, rep from * around (64 sts).

Third dec row: Ch 1, (working each st instead of sp) sk first st, * work 1 sc in each of next 5 sts, sc2tog , rep from * 8 times more (9 dec in all) (55 sts), join with Sl st to beg ch 1, do not fasten off yarn (this is center back of cap).

FINISHING
1. Pin bill to cap front edge, right sides together, matching centers. Sew pieces together using tapestry needle and long yarn that was left, weave in ends.
2. Pick up yarn at center back, sc along bottom of cap, around edge of bill, and back to where you started. Join with Sl st, fasten off, weave in ends using tapestry needle.

Super Bulky Hat

Wear this hat on the coldest days of winter. Hooked

from super bulky wool on a large hook, it's quick

and easy to make.

YARN

Super bulky weight wool yarn

Shown: Burly Spun by Brown Sheep, 100% wool, 8 oz (226 g)/132 yd (121 m): #BS-59, 1 skein

HOOK

15/P (10 mm)

STITCH USED

Single crochet

GAUGE

9 sc = 4" (10 cm)

NOTIONS

Stitch marker

Tapestry needle

FINISHED SIZE

20" to 21" (51 to 53.5 cm) head circumference

Single crochet rounds without increases shape the brim.

HAT

Foundation rnd: Ch 6, join with Sl st to form ring. Work 6 sc in ring, pm for beg of rnds, carry marker up at end of each rnd.

Rnd 1: Work 2 sc in each st around (12 sc).

Rnd 2: * Work 1 sc in next st, 2 sc in next st (inc made), rep from * around (18 sc).

Rnd 3: * Work 1 sc in each of next 2 sts, 2 sc in next st, rep from * around (24 sc).

Rnd 4: * Work 1 sc in each of next 3 sts, 2 sc in next st, rep from * around (30 sc).

Rnd 5: * Work 1 sc in each of next 4 sts, 2 sc in next st, rep from * around (36 sc).

Rnd 6: * Work 1 sc in each of next 5 sts, 2 sc in next st, rep from * around (42 sc).

Rnd 7: * Work 1 sc in each of next 6 sts, 2 sc in next st, rep from * around (48 sc).

Rnd 8: * Work 1 sc in next st, rep from * around (48 sc). Mark this rnd for start of brim.

Rep rnd 8 until brim is 3" (7.5 cm), fasten off.

FINISHING
Weave in ends using tapestry needle. Roll up brim.

Cozy Baby Hat

A baby hat is such a perfect newborn gift that I couldn't resist including just one. This is a super-soft hat with earflaps and a twist on top.

YARN

Lightweight alpaca yarn in two colors

Shown: Indiecita Baby Alpaca DK by Plymouth, 100% superfine baby alpaca, 1.75 oz (50 g)/125 yd (115 m): #3425, 1 skein (A); #100, 1 skein (B)

HOOKS

5/F (3.75 mm)

6/G (4 mm)

STITCHES USED

Single crochet

Single crochet through back loop

Double crochet

Reverse single crochet

GAUGE

9 clusters = 4" (10 cm) using 6/G hook

6 rows of band = 1" (2.5 cm) using 5/F hook

NOTION

Tapestry needle

FINISHED SIZE

14" (35.5 cm) head circumference

Shell-stitch rows in alternating colors form the crown.

HAT

Begin with bottom band as follows:

Foundation row: Using 5/F hook and A, ch 11. Starting in second ch from hook, work 1 sc in each ch to end (10 sc), ch 1 (counts as sc now and throughout), turn.

Row 1: Working tbl, sk first st, work 1 sc in each st across.

Rep row 1 for 84 rows, do not fasten off.

Still using A, pick up 72 sc, evenly spaced, along row ends (long side of band). This will be RS of your work. Ch 1, turn.

Change to 6/G hook and work patt as foll:

Foundation row: Sk first st, work 1 sc in next st, * 1 sc, 1 dc in next st, sk 1, rep from * across, ending 1 sc in tch, ch 2, turn.

Row 1: * Work [1 sc, 1 dc] in next st, rep from * 33 times, end 1 dc in tch (34 CL), ch 1, turn.

Row 2: Work 1 dc in same st as tch, * [1 sc, 1 dc] in next st, rep from * 34 times, end 1 sc in tch (35 CL), do not fasten off A, join B.

Rep rows 1 and 2, alternating A and B every two rows for 12 more rows, ch 1, turn. Fasten off B and complete top shaping with A as foll:

Row 1: * Sc in each of next 8 sts, sc2tog, rep from * across, end 1 sc (65 sts), ch 1, turn.

Row 2: Sk first st, sc in each of next 2 sts, sc2tog, * sc in each of next 5 sts, sc2tog, rep from * across, end 5 sc (56 sts), ch 1, turn.

Row 3: Sk first st, sc2tog, * sc in each of next 3 sts, sc2tog, rep from * across (45 sts), ch 1, turn.

Row 4: Sk first st, sc2tog, * sc in each of next 3 sts, sc2tog, rep from * across (36 sts), ch 1, turn.

Row 5: Sk first st, sc2tog, * sc in each of next 3 sts, sc2tog, rep from * across (29 sts), ch 1, turn.

Row 6: Sk first st, sc2tog, * sc in each of next 3 stitches, sc2tog, rep from * across, end 1 sc (23 sts), ch 1, turn.

Row 7: Sk first st, sc2tog across (12 sts), ch 1, turn.

Row 8: Sc2tog across row, fasten off, leaving long end for sewing.

Single crochet stitches worked through the back loop create a "ribbed" bottom band.

EARLFAPS
Make two.

Foundation row: With A, ch 13. Starting in second ch from hook, work 1 sc in each ch (12 sc), ch 1, turn.

Row 1: Sk first st, work 1 sc in each st across, ch 1, turn.

Rows 2, 3, and 4: Rep row 1.

Row 5: Sk first st, sc2tog, sc to last 3 sts, sc2tog, sc in last st, ch 1, turn.

Row 6: Rep row 1.

Cont to rep rows 5 and 1 until 4 sts rem, sc2tog twice, turn, sc2tog, fasten off, leaving long end for sewing.

TOP TWISTS
Make four.

Using double strand of any leftover yarn, ch 25, turn, work 2 sc in each ch, fasten off, leaving a long end to attach to top of hat.

FINISHING

1. Sew the back seam of the hat, using a tapestry needle and the long yarn that was left, weave in end.

2. Fold the bottom band in half to the inside, and sew in place, weave in end.

3. With B and 5/F hook, work 1 row sc into bottom fold of band, do not turn. Work 1 row rev sc around bottom of hat, fasten off, weave in end.

4. Sew the earflaps in place under the reverse crochet row using long yarn that was left, leaving 1" (2.5 cm) space on each side of the back seam. Weave in ends.

5. With B and 5/F hook, starting at top corner of one earflap, RS facing you, pick up 14 sc down to point, ch 45 for tie, work sc up the ch sts, then cont on other side of earflap, fasten off, weave in ends. Rep for the other earflap.

6. Sew twists to top of hat.

Lion's Mane Hood

This fun-fur hood with pom-poms is warm and
sexy. The project goes fast, since it's made with
large hooks.

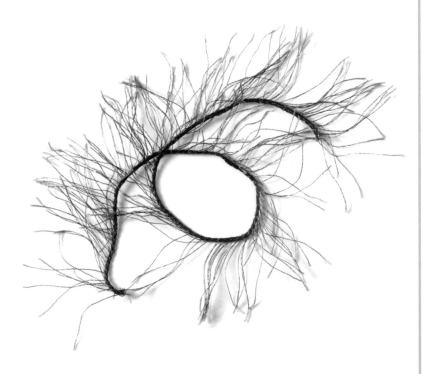

YARN

Bulky-weight novelty fur yarn

Shown: Fun Fur by Lion Brand,
100% polyester, 1.75 oz
(50 g)/ 60 yd (55 m): Copper
#134, 4 balls

Bulky-weight acrylic/wool blend
yarn

Shown: Wool-Ease Chunky by
Lion Brand, 80% acrylic/20%
wool, 5 oz (142 g)/153 yd
(140 m): Pumpkin #133, 1 skein

HOOKS

15/P (10 mm)

9/I (5.5 mm)

STITCH USED

Single crochet

GAUGE

7 sc = 4" (10 cm) on 15/P
hook

NOTIONS

Tapestry needle

3" (7.5 cm) square of cardboard

FINISHED SIZE

20" to 22" (51 to 56 cm)
head circumference

Bulky-weight acrylic/wool blend yarn in single crochet edges the hood.

HOOD

Fur yarn is used double strand throughout.

Foundation row: Starting at bottom back of neck, with eyelash yarn and 15/P hook, ch 6. Work 1 sc in second ch from hook, 1 sc in each ch (5 sc), ch 1, turn.

Row 1: Sk first st, work 1 sc in each st across, ch 1, turn.

Rows 2, 3, and 4: Rep row 1.

Row 5: Sk first st, work 2 sc in next st (inc made), sc to last 2 sts, inc 1, 1 sc in last st (7 sc), ch 1, turn.

Rows 6, 7, and 8: Rep row 1.

Row 9: Rep row 5 (9 sc).

Rows 10, 11, and 12: Rep row 1.

Row 13: Rep row 5 (11 sc).

Rows 14, 15, and 16: Rep row 1. At end of row 16, do not turn, ch 17 sts, turn.

Starting in second ch from hook, sc in each added ch, cont sc in next 11 sts, ch 17 on other side, turn.

Starting in second ch from hook, sc in each added ch, cont sc to end (43 sc)—16 new sts have been added on each side of center panel of 11 sts.

Cont working in sc on all 43 sts for 7" (18 cm) more, fasten off, weave in ends using tapestry needle.

POM-POMS
Make two.

Cut a piece of eyelash yarn about 18" (46 cm) long, for tying pompom; set aside. Cut 3" (7.5 cm) square of firm cardboard. Wrap yarn 120 times around cardboard. Carefully remove wraps from cardboard, and tie securely in center. Cut lps, shake out, and trim to form ball.

FINISHING
1. Hat is T-shaped piece. Fold the horizontal extensions down to meet the vertical sides of the center panel. Sew the edges together.
2. Using 9/I hook and Chunky yarn, leaving a long end to tie on pom-pom, ch 50. Join to left front bottom of hat, continue in sc all around front edge of hat to bottom right front, continue in sc along neck edge back to left front bottom, ch 1, turn. Work a second row back along neck edge. When you reach right front bottom, ch 50, fasten off, leaving a long end to tie on pom-pom.
3. Tie pom-poms to ends of chains.

Cotton Candy
Scarf Hat

It's a scarf, it's a hat, it's both. This

fluffy creation is crocheted in luxurious

mohair yarn in an open pattern.

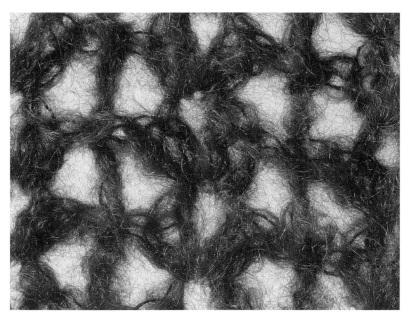
Lacy open-work pattern of double crochet shells and triple crochet stitches.

Make two pieces.

Foundation row: Starting at top, ch 26. Starting in fifth ch from hook, * work 2 dc, ch 2, 2 dc in same ch, sk 2 ch, 1 tr in next ch, sk 2 ch, rep from * until 3 ch rem, sk 2 ch, 1 tr in last ch, ch 4, turn.

Row 1: * Work 2 dc, ch 2, 2 dc in next ch-2 sp, 1 FPtr over bar of tr of prev row, rep from * across, end 1 tr in top of tch, ch 4, turn.

Rep row 1 for 36" (91.5 cm), fasten off.

FINISHING
Using tapestry needle, sew pieces together at top and 10" (25.5 cm) down back. Weave in ends.

YARN
Bulky mohair yarn

Shown: Ingenua by Katia, 78% mohair/13% polyamide/9% wool, 1.75 oz (50 g)/153 yd (140 m): 1 ball

HOOK
10½/K (6.5 mm)

STITCHES USED
Double crochet
Triple crochet
Front post triple crochet

GAUGE
2 shells 2 tr = 4" (10 cm)

NOTIONS
Tapestry needle

FINISHED SIZE
10" × 36" (25.5 × 91.5 cm) head circumference

Peruvian Hat

This colorful, warm ski hat is an intermediate-level

crochet project. The stripes are worked vertically,

and all the colors except the bright accent stripe

(color D) can be carried loosely up the sides as you

hook along. Add tassels to the flaps if you like.

YARN

Lightweight wool yarn in five colors

Shown: Cleckheaton Country by Plymouth, 100% wool, 1.75 oz (50 g)/104 yd (95 m): Light Blue #1935, 1 skein (A); Turquoise #2230, 1 skein (B); Periwinkle #1548, 1 skein (C); Orange #2167, 1 skein (D); Dark Purple #0288, 1 skein (E)

HOOK

8/H (5 mm)

STITCHES USED

Single crochet

Single crochet through back loop

Double crochet

Popcorn

GAUGE

10 sc and 20 rows = 4" (10 cm)

NOTIONS

Stitch marker

Tapestry needle

3½ (9 cm) piece of cardboard

FINISHED SIZE

20" to 21" (51 to 53.5 cm) head circumference

Alternating stripes of single crochet and popcorn stitches.

HAT

Foundation row (WS): Using A, ch 22. Starting in second ch from hook, work 1 sc in each ch to end (21 sc), ch 1, turn.

Row 1: Sk first st, sc in each st across, ch 1, turn.

Row 2 (pc row, worked from WS): Sk first st, work 1 sc in each of next 2 sts, * pc in next st, sc in each of next 3 sts, rep from * across, end last rep with sc in top of tch (5 pc, 3 sc at beg, and bet each pc, 1 sc at end of row), pull up B in last lp, ch 1 with B, turn.

Row 3: With B, sk first st, work 1 sc in each st across row, 1 sc in top of tch, ch 1, turn.

Row 4: Sk first st, work 1 sc in each st across, 1 sc in top of tch, turn. Pull up C in last lp, ch 1 with C, do not end A.

Row 5: With C, sk first st, work 1 sc tbl only in each st across, ch 1, turn.

Row 6: Sk first st, work 1 sc in each st across, pull up B in last st, do not end C, ch 1 with B, turn.

Row 7: With B, sk first st, work 1 sc in each st across, 1 sc in top of tch, ch 1, turn.

Row 8: Rep row 2, except pull up E in last st, do not end B, turn.

Rows 9–20: Rep rows 3 and 4, alternating colors E, C, E, A, D, B every other row. When changing yarns, fasten off only yarn D. At end of row 20, pull up C in last lp, ch 1 with C, turn.

Row 21: With C, rep row 3.

Row 22: With C, rep row 2, pull up E in last lp, do not end C, ch 1 with E, turn.

Rows 23–30: Rep rows 3 and 4, alternating colors E, A, B, A, every other row.

Rep rows 1–30 twice more (90 rows in all), fasten off.

Using tapestry needle, sew back seam.

CROWN

Rnd 1: With RS facing, starting at top seam, join C, working in sc, work 1 rnd, picking up 1 sc every other row (45 sc), pm in work to mark beg of rnds.

Rnd 2: Work 1 sc in each st around.

Rnd 3: * Work 1 sc in each of next 2 sts, sc2tog, rep from * around, end 1 sc (34 sc).

Rnd 4: * Work 1 sc in next st, sc2tog, rep from * around, end 1 sc (23 sc).

Rnd 5: * Sc2tog, rep from * around, end 1 sc (11 sc), fasten off, leaving long end for sewing.

Using tapestry needle, gather top, sew securely, fasten off.

Using C, work 1 row sc around bottom of hat, set aside.

Shell pattern finishes edge of hat and earflaps.

EARFLAPS
Make two.

With B, ch 17. Work 4 rows sc, then dec 1 st each side every other row until 4 sts rem. Ch 1, turn, sc2tog, 1 sc, ch 1 turn, pick up lp in each of next 2 sts, work off all 3 lps tog. Fasten off B.

With D, starting at top corner, with RS facing, work sc down to point, 3 sc in point to turn, sc back to top, fasten off

TASSELS
Using 1 strand of each color, wind yarn around a 3¹/₂" (9 cm) piece of cardboard once, tie at top, leaving a long end to attach to bottom of earflaps. Tie ¹/₂" (1.3 cm) down from first tie, leaving a long enough end to become part of the tassel.

FINISHING
1. Sew earflaps in place at bottom of hat, leaving 2" (5 cm) space at center back.
2. With C, starting at back seam, work 1 row sc along back, down one side of earflap, 3 sc in corner, up other side of earflap, along front edge of hat,

around other earflap, continuing back to where you started. Do not fasten off, do not turn.

3. Continuing along sts previously worked, work shell patt as foll: * Sk 1 st, work 3 dc in next st, sk 1 st, 1 sc next st, rep from * around bottom of hat and earflaps.

4. Weave in all ends and tie tassels to bottom of earflaps.

Crochet Stitches

SLIP KNOT AND CHAIN

All crochet begins with a chain, into which is worked the foundation row for your piece. To make a chain, start with a slip knot. To make a slip knot, make a loop several inches from the end of the yarn, insert the hook through the loop, and catch the tail with the end **(1).** Draw the yarn through the loop on the hook **(2).** After the slip knot, start your chain. Wrap the yarn over the hook (yarn over) and catch it with the hook. Draw the yarn through the loop on the hook. You have now made 1 chain.

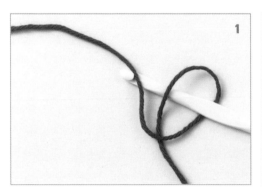
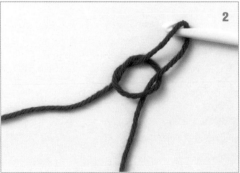

Repeat the process to make a row of chains. When counting chains, do not count the slip knot at the beginning or the loop that is on the hook **(3).**

SLIP STITCH

The slip stitch is a very short stitch, which is mainly used to join two pieces of crochet together when working in rounds. To make a slip stitch, insert the hook into the specified stitch, wrap the yarn over the hook **(1),** and then draw the yarn through the stitch and the loop already on the hook **(2).**

SINGLE CROCHET

Insert the hook into the specified stitch, wrap the yarn over the hook, and draw the yarn through the stitch so there are 2 loops on the hook **(1).** Wrap the yarn over the hook again and draw the yarn through both loops **(2).** When working in single crochet, always insert the hook through both top loops of the next stitch, unless the directions specify front loop or back loop only.

SINGLE CROCHET TWO STITCHES TOGETHER

This decreases the number of stitches in a row or round by 1. Insert the hook into the specified stitch, wrap the yarn over the hook, and draw the yarn through the stitch so there are 2 loops on the hook **(1).** Insert the hook through the next stitch, wrap the yarn over the hook, and draw the yarn through the stitch so there are 3 loops on the hook **(2).** Wrap the yarn over the hook again and draw the yarn through all the loops at once.

 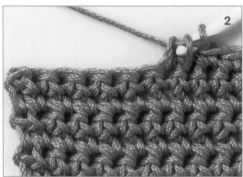

SINGLE CROCHET THROUGH THE BACK LOOP

This creates a distinct ridge on the side facing you. Insert the hook through the back loop only of each stitch, rather than under both loops of the stitch. Complete the single crochet as usual.

REVERSE SINGLE CROCHET

This stitch is usually used to create a border. At the end of a row, chain 1 but do not turn. Working backward, insert the hook into the previous stitch **(1),** wrap the yarn over the hook, and draw the yarn through the stitch so there are 2 loops on the hook. Wrap the yarn over the hook again and draw the yarn through both loops. Continue working in the reverse direction **(2).**

HALF DOUBLE CROCHET

Wrap the yarn over the hook, insert the hook into the specified stitch, and wrap the yarn over the hook again **(1).** Draw the yarn through the stitch so there are 3 loops on the hook. Wrap the yarn over the hook and draw it through all 3 loops at once **(2).**

DOUBLE CROCHET

Wrap the yarn over the hook, insert the hook into the specified stitch, and wrap the yarn over the hook again. Draw the yarn through the stitch so there are 3 loops on the hook **(1).** Wrap the yarn over the hook again and draw it through 2 of the loops so there are now 2 loops on the hook **(2).** Wrap the yarn over the hook again and draw it through the last 2 loops **(3).**

DOUBLE CROCHET TWO STITCHES TOGETHER

This decreases the number of stitches in a row or round by 1. Wrap the yarn over the hook, insert the hook into the specified stitch, and wrap the yarn over the hook again. Draw the yarn through the stitch so there are 3 loops on the hook. Wrap the yarn over the hook again and draw in through 2 of the loops so there are now 2 loops on the hook. Wrap the yarn over the hook and pick up a loop in the next stitch, so there are now 4 loops on the hook. Wrap the yarn over the hook and draw through 2 loops, yarn over and draw through 3 loops to complete the stitch.

DOUBLE CROCHET THROUGH THE BACK LOOP

This creates a distinct ridge on the side facing you. Wrap the yarn over the hook and insert the hook through the back loop only of each stitch, rather than under both loops of the stitch. Complete the double crochet as usual.

TRIPLE CROCHET

Wrap the yarn over the hook twice, insert the hook into the specified stitch, and wrap the yarn over the hook again. Draw the yarn through the stitch so there are 4 loops on the hook. Wrap the yarn over the hook again **(1)** and draw it through 2 of the loops so there are now 3 loops on the hook **(2).** Wrap the yarn over the hook again and draw it through 2 of the loops so there are now 2 loops on the hook **(3).** Wrap the yarn over the hook again and draw it through the last 2 loops **(4).**

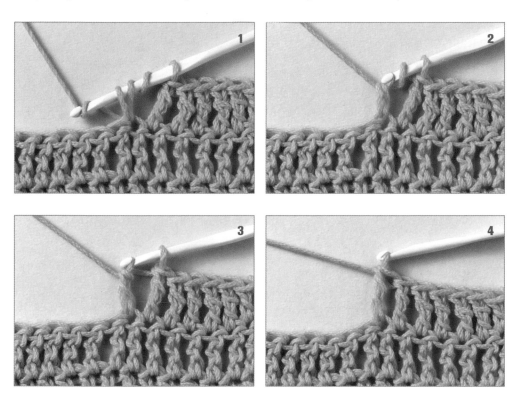

POPCORN STITCH 1

(Worked from the wrong side): Wrap the yarn over the hook, pick up a loop in the next stitch, yarn over and through 2 loops **(1)**. [Wrap the yarn over the hook, pick up a loop in the same stitch, yarn over and through 2 loops] 2 times. Wrap the yarn over the hook and draw it through all 4 loops on the hook **(2)**.

FRONT POST DOUBLE CROCHET

This stitch follows a row of double crochet.

Chain 3 to turn. Wrap the yarn over the hook. Working from the front, insert the hook from right to left (left to right for left-handed crocheters) under the post of the first double crochet from the previous row, and pick up a loop (shown). Wrap the yarn over the hook and complete the stitch as a double crochet.

Left-handed.

Right-handed.

FRONT POST TRIPLE CROCHET

Wrap the yarn over the hook twice. Working from the front, insert the hook from right to left (left to right for left-handed crocheters) under the post of the indicated stitch in the row below, and pick up a loop (shown). Wrap the yarn over the hook and complete the triple crochet stitch as usual.

Left-handed.

Right-handed.

Abbreviations

approx	approximately		**patt**	pattern
beg	begin/beginning		**pc**	popcorn
bet	between		**pm**	place marker
BL	back loop(s)		**prev**	previous
BP	back post		**rem**	remain/remaining
BPdc	back post double crochet		**rep**	repeat(s)
CC	contrasting color		**rev sc**	reverse single crochet
ch	chain		**rnd(s)**	round(s)
ch-	refers to chain or space previously made, e.g., ch-1 space		**RS**	right side(s)
ch lp	chain loop		**sc**	single crochet
ch-sp	chain space		**sc2tog**	single crochet 2 stitches together
CL	cluster(s)		**sk**	skip
cm	centimeter(s)		**Sl st**	slip stitch
cont	continue		**sp(s)**	space(s)
dc	double crochet		**st(s)**	stitch(es)
dc2tog	double crochet 2 stitches together		**tch**	turning chain
dec	decrease/decreases/decreasing		**tbl**	through back loop
FL	front loop(s)		**tog**	together
foll	follow/follows/following		**tr**	triple crochet
FP	front post		**WS**	wrong side(s)
FPdc	front post double crochet		**yd**	yard(s)
FPtr	front post triple crochet		**yo**	yarn over
g	gram(s)		**yoh**	yarn over hook
hdc	half double crochet		**[ ]**	Work instructions within brackets as many times as directed
inc	increase/increases/increasing		**( )**	At end of row, indicates total number of stitches worked
lp(s)	loop(s)		*****	Repeat instructions following the single asterisk as directed
m	meter(s)		******	Repeat instructions between asterisks as many times as directed or repeat from a given set of instructions
MC	main color			
mm	millimeter(s)			
oz	ounce(s)			
p	picot			